Ballad for the Unsung Poets of the Ages

KOSTAS KARYOTAKIS

Ballad for the Unsung Poets of the Ages

SELECTED POEMS AND PROSE

Translated by
Simon Darragh

Introduction by
Dimitris Daskalopoulos

AIORA

For Simon

Simon Darragh was a poet and translator. He translated among other things the works of Nikos Kavvadias. *Foreign Correspondence* (Peterloo, 2000) is a volume of Darragh's own poetry. Darragh was a Hawthornden Fellow, and a Translator in Residence at the University of East Anglia. He lived in the Northern Sporades for 25 years. He died in 2023.

© Aiora Press 2024

All rights reserved. No part of this publication may be reproduced, stored in a retrieval system, or transmitted, in any form or by any means, electronic, mechanical, photocopying, recording or otherwise, without written permission of the publishers.

ISBN: 978-618-5369-80-4

First edition January 2024
Reprinted February 2025

AIORA PRESS
11 Mavromichali st.
Athens 10679 - Greece
tel: +30 210 3839000
www.aiorabooks.com

Contents

INTRODUCTION 9

SELECTED POEMS

The Suffering of Man and of Objects
- Night 19

Népenthè
- Don Quixotes 23
- Polyhymnia 25
- Ballad for the Unsung Poets of the Ages 29
- Tree 33
- Stanzas 1–10 35
- The Moon Tonight 55
- Only 57

Elegies and Satires
- Final Journey 59
- All Together 61
- Ideal Suicides 63
- Michalios 65
- Yellow Spirochete 67

Little Un-symphony in A-Major 69
Career 71
Posthumus
Preveza 73
SELECTED PROSE
An Opportune Death 79
The Skull 83
The Garden of Ingratitude 89
The Last Letter 93
CHRONOLOGY 97
INDEX OF GREEK TITLES 101

Introduction

The reception and wider recognition of Karyotakis' poetry stands typically as a case of belated reaction and faulty aesthetic appreciation. Among the most significant Greek poets of the interwar period, Konstantinos Karyotakis (who signed himself K.G. Karyotakis) was for a long period undervalued and misconstrued. Some fifty years would need to elapse for him to be accorded his rightful place in twentieth-century Greek poetry.

He was born in Tripoli, Peloponnese, on 30 October 1896, but never lived there: Tripoli was just one in a series of postings—a feature then of civil service life—for his father, who was a county engineer. In his boyhood and adolescence the poet-to-be spent stretches of time in Lefkas, Argostoli, Patras, Larisa, Kalamata, Athens and Chania, the latter being where he completed his schooling. It was there too that he experienced unrequited love with an older girl. Those who knew him as a

pupil remembered a shy, introverted boy, who was often the target of bullying. While still at school he began to publish some juvenilia, along with puzzles and riddles, in popular and youth periodicals. He learnt fluent French and passable German and later on these would serve him to translate French and German poetry. He attended the Athens University Law School, receiving his degree in 1917, with the aim of setting up as a lawyer. He soon quit law, however, and followed in his father's footsteps by joining the civil service and embarking on a series of postings himself, experiencing at first hand the often duplicitous and self-serving ways of his colleagues. His postings, sequentially, were in Thessaloniki, Syros, Arta, Athens, Patras and Preveza.

During his stint in Athens he became acquainted with poet Maria Polydouri (1902–30) who was his colleague for a while. Others viewed his friendship with and feelings for her as an unrequited romance, and occasionally a torrid love affair, but this did not reflect reality. Polydouri led *la vie bohème*, in a self-destructive bent, and was stricken with consumption. She died extremely young, just a couple of years after Karyotakis, having inspired lovelorn feelings in other poets her age. According to Charilaos Sakellariadis, Karyotakis' very close friend and original publisher, 'this short-lived and much misunderstood friendship was only an emotional episode', but served as the occasion for 'several imprecisions and improprieties' to be written about the two unfortunate poets.

Karyotakis and Sakellariades jointly composed a revue in 1921, entitled 'Pell-Mell', but it was never staged. Karyotakis made a few short trips to other European countries—Germany, Italy (Rome and Venice), France (Paris) and Romania—and it was thought by some that on one of those trips he contracted an STD, chiefly on account of his poem 'Yellow Spirochete'. But according to later views his problem was not a disease, but the use of narcotics.

His output consists of three poetry collections, a few translations and some prose pieces. His official debut in literature was in 1919, with his short poetry collection *The Suffering of Man and of Objects*. The same year, along with his friend Agis Levendis, he published *The Leg*, a weekly literary-satirical review, which was considered too audacious and ceased publication following its sixth issue. Nonetheless, in its short run, many well-known writers contributed. Karyotakis also contributed poems and satirical prose pieces, signing either with his surname or one of several noms de plume. In fact, as many who knew him have written, the poet was a resourceful practical joker and several of his exploits have been recorded. In 1920 he was awarded a prize in the Philadelphian poetry competition for poems he had submitted under the title *Songs of the Motherland*, some of which were subsequently included in *Népenthè*, his second poetry collection (1921). In 1927 he brought out his third collection, which was entitled *Elegies and Satires*. In 1928, due to his involvement with trade-unionist civil

service activism he was transferred to Preveza where, on 21 July, he took his own life.

The tragic end of his life was very much talked about by young people at the time (there were some sporadic copycat suicides) and a trend emerged of morbid versifying and literary emulation going by the name of 'karyotakismos', but it disappeared after a while without leaving any significant literary work. The important thing is that Karyotakis' suicide brought this rather neglected poet to the limelight, promoting him as someone who stood out in the era's mediocre poetic production. It also set a hallmark of sincerity and authenticity on his output. His personal misadventures, the fixation with death in many of his verses, and the marked satirical slant of his poems, which occasionally turns to self-deprecation, managed to transform his individual drama into 'an active metaphor of human destiny'.

The 1920s, the decade in which Karyotakis produced his poetry, translations and prose, were marked by a sequence of momentous developments for Greece, with continually alternating governments and coups. The Asia Minor Disaster put paid to an initial optimistic outlook regarding the campaign there, and created the enormous social problem of homing the refugees. Politics did not leave him indifferent, as can be seen in several of his poems such as 'Michalios', 'To the Statue of Liberty that illumines the world', 'To Andreas Calvos' and 'The plain and the cemetery'. His poems encompass realism and

symbolism, and also show the influences of chiefly French poets, such as Jean Moréas, Charles Baudelaire and José Maria Hérédia. His poetry, as was the case with a large number of his peers, has as its main themes erotic love and death, and is imbued with a pronounced air of pessimism and a manifest painful suffering arising from a life lacking fulfilment. He countered personal difficulties with caustic language and irony. In both his social and civil service surroundings he had a feeling that his life was that of an automaton, utterly alien to his deeper disposition and his artistic idiosyncrasy.

Ten years after Karyotakis' suicide, Charilaos Sakellariadis edited an omnibus edition of the poet's work, under the title *Collected Works, Verse and Prose*. He included two pieces of criticism that had been written while the poet was still alive. This is not a literary edition, but stands as a friendly gesture, of a practical nature, that preserves information and interesting particulars about the life of the poet, some of a somewhat anecdotal character. The assimilation of his poetry by the broader public, arising from this edition, would be put on pause by the Second World War, and the foreign occupation of Greece that followed, and the civil war that came after that. A substantial reassessment of his work arose in the 1960s, when a two-volume literary edition edited by G. P. Savvidis was published as *Apanda ta Evriskomena* [Collected Works]. This was followed by several extensive papers and articles in periodicals about his life and work. Since then an ever-expanding literature has yielded,

among other things, an extensive chronology of his life and times, a tabulated glossary culled from his poems, a draft bibliography and scholarly congresses regarding his overall output. It was high time for a stop to be put to 'this indescribable motley of biographical tid-bits, police-beat reporting, and clinical gossip that obscures our view of the poet's output [...] In other words: it is time to desist from occupying ourselves with Karyotakis' spirochete, still less with his suicide, and to turn to his poetry and prose'.

The concerted work of scholars on Karyotakis' output since the 1960s has rebutted many of the earlier prevailing views, particularly as regards his relations to the modernist Generation of the Thirties. Apropos of a very few early and contentious pieces by certain exponents of that generation, scholars believed the Generation of the Thirties viewed Karyotakis adversarially, but this is a view that is not borne out based on the writings of those representing that generation. Quite the reverse, there has been a thorough exploration of several emblematic poets of the Thirties and there are clear reverberations of the Karyotakis strain. At the same time his influence has been remarked among later poets, including those of our times.

We can safely say at this point that the case of K.G. Karyotakis, poet, who never abandoned verse composition, signalled the end of this traditional poetic expression, prior to the emergence of modernism—though it

did not in itself mark the arrival of modernist poetry in Greece (as had been maintained in the past). With his output, Karyotakis holds a special position between tradition and free verse, and remains an active force in contemporary Greek poetry.

Dimitris Daskalopoulos

Translated by
Alexander Zaphiriou

Selected Poems

ΝΥΧΤΑ

Εἶναι ἀξημέρωτη νύχτα ἡ ζωή.

Στὶς μεσονύχτιες στράτες περπατᾶνε
ἀποσταμένοι οἱ ἔρωτες
κι οἱ γρίλιες τῶν παράθυρων ἐστάξανε
τὸν πόνο ποὺ κρατᾶνε.

Στὶς στέγες ἐκρεμάστη τὸ φεγγάρι
σκυμμένο πρὸς τὰ δάκρυά του
κι ἡ μυρωμένη λύπη τῶν τριαντάφυλλων
τὸ δρόμο της θὰ πάρει.

Ὁλόρθο τὸ φανάρι μας σωπαίνει
χλωμὸ καὶ μυστηριώδικο
κι ἡ πόρτα τοῦ σπιτιοῦ μου εἶναι σὰ ν' ἄνοιξε
καὶ λείψανο νὰ βγαίνει.

Σαρκάζει τὸ κρεβάτι τὴ χαρά τους
κι αὐτοὶ λὲν πὼς ἔτριξε·
δὲ λὲν πὼς τὸ κρεβάτι ὁραματίζεται
μελλοντικοὺς θανάτους.

Καὶ κλαῖνε οἱ ἀμανέδες στὶς ταβέρνες
τὴ νύχτα τὴν ἀστρόφεγγη

NIGHT

Life is a dawnless night.

Wearily loves walk
the midnight streets
and the slats of the window-blinds
drip their pain.

Hung on the roof-tops, the moon
bends to its tears
and the roses' sad scent will soon
make its farewell.

Upright, the street-lamp says nothing
mysterious, pale
and the door of my house seems to open
to bring forth a corpse.

The bed smirks at their joy
and they say it creaks;
they don't say the bed can foresee
future deaths.

And the sad songs weep in the taverns
the starry night long—

ποὺ θά 'πρεπε ἡ ἀγάπη νὰν τὴν ἔπινε
καὶ παίζουν οἱ λατέρνες.

Χυμένες στὰ ποτήρια καρτεροῦνε
οἱ λησμονιὲς γλυκύτατες·
οἱ χίμαιρες τώρα θὰ εἰποῦν τὸ λόγο τους
καὶ οἱ ἄνθρωποι θ' ἀκοῦνε.

Καθημερνῶν χαμῶνε κοιμητήρι
τὸ πάρκον ἀνατρίχιασε
τὴν ὥρα ποὺ νεκρὸς κάποιος ἐκίνησε
νὰ πάει στὴ χλόη νὰ γείρει.

love should have drunk the night—
and the street-organs play.

Poured into glasses, forgotten
sweetness endures;
now the chimeras will speak
people shall hear.

The graveyard of each day's perdition
shivered the plot
at the hour when some dead man set out
to lie with the grass.

ΔΟΝ ΚΙΧΩΤΕΣ

Οἱ Δὸν Κιχῶτες πᾶνε ὀμπρὸς καὶ βλέπουνε ὡς τὴν ἄκρη
τοῦ κονταριοῦ ποὺ ἐκρέμασαν σημαία τους τὴν Ἰδέα.
Κοντόφθαλμοι ὁραματιστές, ἕνα δὲν ἔχουν δάκρυ
γιὰ νὰ δεχτοῦν ἀνθρώπινα κάθε βρισιὰ χυδαία.

Σκοντάφτουνε στὴ Λογικὴ καὶ στὰ ραβδιὰ τῶν ἄλλων
ἀστεῖα δαρμένοι σέρνονται καταμεσὶς τοῦ δρόμου,
ὁ Σάντσος λέει «δὲ σ' τὸ 'λεγα;» μὰ ἐκεῖνοι τῶν μεγάλων
σχεδίων, ἀντάξιοι μένουνε καί: «Σάντσο, τ' ἄλογό μου!»

Ἔτσι ἂν τὸ θέλει ὁ Θερβάντες, ἐγὼ τοὺς εἶδα, μέσα
στὴν μίαν ἀνάλγητη Ζωή, τοῦ Ὀνείρου τοὺς ἱππότες
ἄναντρα νὰ πεζέψουνε καί, μὲ πικρὴν ἀνέσα,
μὲ μάτια ὀγρά, τὶς χίμαιρες ν' ἀπαρνηθοῦν τὶς πρῶτες.

Τοὺς εἶδα πίσω νά 'ρθουνε—παράφρονες, ὡραῖοι
ρηγάδες ποὺ ἐπολέμησαν γι' ἀνύπαρχτο βασίλειο—
καὶ σὰν πορφύρα νιώθοντας χλευαστικιά, πῶς ρέει,
τὴν ἀνοιχτὴ νὰ δείξουνε μάταιη πληγὴ στὸν ἥλιο!

DON QUIXOTES

The Don Quixotes advance, see as far as the tip
of the spear where their Idea hangs like a flag.
Short-sighted visionaries, they shed not a tear
as they take in the people's vulgar curse.

They stumble on Reason, on others' sticks,
beaten clown-like they crawl down the road,
Sancho says, 'Well I told you', but they live up
to their grandiose plans: 'Sancho, my horse!'

If Cervantes wishes, then so I see them,
in a heartless Life, knights of the Dream,
cowardly dismounting, with bitter ease,
eyes wet, they renounce the first chimeras.

I saw them come back—lunatic, handsome
kings who fought for an unreal kingdom—
like purple they feel their mocking blood run,
vain open wound to show to the sun!

ΠΟΛΥΜΝΙΑ

Ψεύτικα αἰσθήματα
ψεύτη τοῦ κόσμου!
Μὰ τὸ παράξενο
φῶς τοῦ ἔρωτός μου
φέγγει στοῦ σκοτεινοῦ
δρόμου τὴν ἄκρη:
Μὲ τὸ παράπονο
καὶ μὲ τὸ δάκρυ,
κόρη χλωμόθωρη
μαυροντυμένη.
Κι εἶναι σὰν αἴνιγμα,
καὶ περιμένει.
Λάμπει τὸ βλέμμα της
ἀπ' τὴν ἀσθένεια.
Σάμπως νὰ λιώνουνε
χέρια κερένια.
Στ' ἄσαρκα μάγουλα
πῶς ἔχει μείνει
πίκρα τὸ νόημα
γέλιου ποὺ σβήνει!
Εἶναι τὸ ἀξήγητο
τὸ μικροστόμα
δίχως τὸ μίλημα,
δίχως τὸ χρῶμα.

POLYHYMNIA

Lying feelings
liar of the world!
But the strange
light of my love
shines at the dark
edge of the road:
with the complaint
and with the tear,
pale-figured daughter
dressed in black;
And she waits,
like an enigma.
Out of her gaze
sickliness shines.
The waxen hands
seem to melt.
On fleshless cheeks
how it remains,
the bitter sense
of laughter that dies!
The unexplaining
little mouth
without its speech,
without its colour.

Κάποια μεσάνυχτα
θὰ σὲ ἀγαπήσω,
Μοῦσα. Τὰ μάτια σου
θᾶν τὰ φιλήσω,
νά 'βρω γυρεύοντας
μὲς στὰ νερά τους
τὰ χρυσονείρατα
καὶ τοὺς θανάτους,
καὶ τὴ βασίλισσα
λέξη τοῦ κόσμου,
καὶ τὸ παράξενο
φῶς τοῦ ἔρωτός μου.

On some midnight
I shall love you,
Muse. Your eyes
I shall kiss,
seeking to find
in their waters
the golden dreams
and the deaths
and the queen
word of the world
and the strange
light of my love.

ΜΠΑΛΑΝΤΑ ΣΤΟΥΣ ΑΔΟΞΟΥΣ ΠΟΙΗΤΕΣ ΤΩΝ ΑΙΩΝΩΝ

Ἀπὸ θεοὺς κι ἀνθρώπους μισημένοι,
σὰν ἄρχοντες ποὺ ἐξέπεσαν πικροί,
μαραίνονται οἱ Βερλαίν· τοὺς ἀπομένει
πλοῦτος ἡ ρίμα πλούσια καὶ ἀργυρή.
Οἱ Οὐγκὸ μὲ «Τιμωρίες» τὴν τρομερὴ
τῶν Ὀλυμπίων ἐκδίκηση μεθοῦνε.
Μὰ ἐγὼ θὰ γράψω μία λυπητερὴ
μπαλάντα στοὺς ποιητὲς ἄδοξοι πού 'ναι.

Ἂν ἔζησαν οἱ Πόε δυστυχισμένοι,
καὶ ἂν οἱ Μπωντλαὶρ ἐζήσανε νεκροί,
ἡ Ἀθανασία τοὺς εἶναι χαρισμένη.
Κανένας ὅμως δὲν ἀνιστορεῖ
καὶ τὸ ἔρεβος ἐσκέπασε βαρὺ
τοὺς στιχουργοὺς ποὺ ἀνάξια στιχουργοῦνε.
Μὰ ἐγὼ σὰν προσφορὰ κάνω ἱερὴ
μπαλάντα στοὺς ποιητὲς ἄδοξοι πού 'ναι.

Τοῦ κόσμου ἡ καταφρόνια τοὺς βαραίνει
κι αὐτοὶ περνοῦνε ἀλύγιστοι κι ὠχροί,
στὴν τραγικὴ ἀπάτη τους δομένοι
πὼς κάπου πέρα ἡ Δόξα καρτερεῖ,
παρθένα βαθυστόχαστα ἱλαρή.

BALLAD FOR THE UNSUNG POETS OF THE AGES

Hated by gods and mankind,
like nobles bitter in downfall,
the Verlaines wither; they keep
only the rich, silver rhyme.
The Hugos with terrible 'Châtiments'
are drunk on Olympian judgement.
But I shall write a sad
ballad for unsung poets.

What though the Poes lived in misery,
and the Baudelaires lived in death?
They were granted their immortality,
but no-one tells the story
of those now decked by Erebus,
the unworthy poetasters,
but here I offer the holy
ballad for unsung poets.

People's disdain weighs them down
they continue unbending and pale,
given to tragic delusion
that somewhere glory is waiting,
joyful, pure, deeply judged.

Μὰ ξέροντας πὼς ὅλοι τους ξεχνοῦνε,
νοσταλγικὰ ἐγὼ κλαίω τὴ θλιβερὴ
μπαλάντα στοὺς ποιητὲς ἄδοξοι πού 'ναι.

Καὶ κάποτε οἱ μελλούμενοι καιροί:
«Ποιὸς ἄδοξος ποιητής» θέλω νὰ ποῦνε
«τὴν ἔγραψε μίαν ἔτσι πενιχρὴ
μπαλάντα στοὺς ποιητὲς ἄδοξοι πού 'ναι;»

But knowing that all forget them,
nostalgic, I cry the piteous
ballad for unsung poets.

And some time in years to come
I want them to say, 'What unsung
poet wrote that paltry
ballad for unsung poets?'

ΔΕΝΤΡΟ

Μὲ ἀδιάφορο τὸ μέτωπο καὶ πρᾶο,
τὰ δείλια, τὶς αὐγὲς θὰ χαιρετάω.

Δέντρο θὰ στέκομαι, ὅμοια νὰ κοιτάζω
τὴ θύελλαν ἢ τὸν οὐρανὸ γαλάζο.

Εἶναι ζωή, θὰ λέω, τὸ φέρετρο ὅπου
λύπη, χαρὰ τελειώνουνε τοῦ ἀνθρώπου.

TREE

Brow smooth and with gentle mien
I shall greet the sunset and the dawn.

A tree I shall stand, and see the storm
or the clear blue sky the same.

Life's the coffin, I shall say, where Man buries
all his joys, all his sorrows.

ΣΤΡΟΦΕΣ

1

Εἴκοσι χρόνια παίζοντας
ἀντὶ χαρτιὰ βιβλία,
εἴκοσι χρόνια παίζοντας,
ἔχασα τὴ ζωή.
Φτωχὸς τώρα ξαπλώνομαι,
μίαν εὔκολη σοφία
ν' ἀκούσω ἐδῶ ποὺ πλάτανος
γέρος μου τὴ θροεῖ.

STANZAS

1

Twenty years playing
books instead of cards—
twenty years playing.
I mislaid life.
Now, poor, I lie down
here where an old plane tree
murmurs to me
an easy wisdom.

2

Ἀπ' ὅλα θέλω ἐλεύτερος
νὰ πλέω στὰ χάη τοῦ κόσμου.
Ἂν ἕνας φίλος μοῦ 'μεινε,
νὰ φύγει, νὰ περάσει.
Κι ὅταν ζητήσει ὁ θάνατος
τὰ πλούτη πὄχω μάσει,
σένα, πικρία μου ἀπέραντη,
μονάχο νά 'χω βιός μου.

2

Free from all, I want
to float on the world's chaos.
If I still had a friend,
let him leave, let him pass.
And when death asks for
the riches I have amassed,
you, my boundless bitterness,
you will be all I have to show.

3

Γιὰ τὴ ζωή σου μοῦ 'λεγες,
γιὰ τὸ χαμὸ τῆς νιότης,
γιὰ τὴν ἀγάπη μας ποὺ κλαίει
τὸν ἴδιο θάνατό της,
κι ἐνῷ μία ὀγρὴ στὰ μάτια σου
περνοῦσε ἀναλαμπή,
ἥλιος φαιδρὸς ἀπ' τ' ἀνοιχτὸ
παράθυρο εἶχε μπεῖ.

3

You told me of your life,
of the loss of youth,
of our love which laments
its own death,
and, as a flashing tear
passed in your eyes,
a cheerful sun
broke through the window.

4

Τί χάνω ἐγὼ τὶς μέρες μου
τὴ μία κοντὰ στὴν ἄλλη,
κι ὅπως μοῦ ἀσπρίζουν τὰ μαλλιὰ
ξινίζει τὸ κρασί,
ἀφοῦ μονάχα ὅταν περνῶ
τὸ βλέμμα ἀπὸ κρουστάλλι,
μὲ νέα ρετσίνα ὁλόγεμο
βλέπω τὴ ζωὴ χρυσή;

4

Why do I lose my days,
each one so near the next,
and just as my hair turns white
so the wine sours,
since only when my gaze
passes through crystal
brimful of young retsina
do I see life golden?

5

Ἡ νύχτα μᾶς ἐχώρισεν
ἀπὸ ὅσους ἀγαπᾶμε
πρὶν μᾶς χωρίσει ἡ ξενιτιά.
(Νά 'ναι ὅλοι ἐκεῖ στὸ μόλο;)
Σφῦρα, καράβι ἀργήσαμε.
κι ἂν φτάσουμε ὅπου πᾶμε,
στάσου λίγο, μὰ ὕστερα
σφῦρα νὰ φεύγουμε ὅλο.

5

Night parted us
from those we love
before exile parts us.
(Are they all there on the quay?)
Whistle, boat, we're late.
And if we arrive where we're going,
wait a while, but then
whistle for us to leave.

6

Λεῦκες, γιγάντιοι καρφωτοὶ
στὰ πλάγια ἐδῶ τοῦ δρόμου,
δέντρα μου, ἐστέρξατε ὁ βοριὰς
τὰ φύλλα σας νὰ πάρει.
Σκιὲς ἐμείνατε σκιῶν
ποὺ ρέουν στὸ μέτωπό μου,
καθὼς πηγαίνω χάμου ἐγὼ
κι ἀπάνω τὸ φεγγάρι.

6

Poplars, giants stuck here
at the roadside,
my trees, you suffered the north wind
to take your leaves.
Shadows you remain, of shadows
that run on my forehead
as I go on below
and the moon above.

7

Χαρά! Ἡ χαρά! Στὰ νέα χαρὰ
παιδιά! Τραβοῦνε—ὡραῖοι
μαῦροι ληστὲς—τὴν κόρη ζωὴ
δεμένη ν' ἀγαπήσουν.
Μὰ στὸ βιβλίο σου ὁλάνοιχτο,
στὰ φύλλα του αὔρα πνέει,
τρελέ, τρελέ, ποὺ ἐγέρασες
καὶ νέος ποτὲ δὲν ἤσουν.

7

Joy! Joy! To new joy,
children! They drag—handsome
black brigands—the young girl life
tied up to love her.
But your book is all open,
breeze blows on its pages,
fool, fool, who grew old
and were never young.

8

— Ποιητή, κυλάει τὸ γέλιο σου
μέλι καὶ χλεύη, ἀλλὰ
δὲν παύεις νὰ σφυροκοπᾷς
τῶν ἤχων τὰ στεφάνια
— Κόρη, δουλεύω ἀνώφελα,
μὰ ἡ στείρα τί ὠφελᾶ
καὶ σιωπηλὴ τοῦ ἀχάτινου
ματιοῦ σου ὑπερηφάνια;

8

— Poet, your laugh rolls,
honey and mockery, but
you don't stop hammering
the laurels of sound.
— Damsel, I work fruitlessly,
but of what use is the sterile
and silent pride
of your agate eye?

9

Ἀντίο! Ἀντίο! Μὲ τὰ οὐράνια
μάτια σας καὶ μὲ βιόλες
στὸ λαιμό, ἐφύγατε, ξανθὲς
ἐρώτων νέων ἐλπίδες.
Ἀντίο, κι ἐσὺ ποὺ στρέφοντας,
ὅταν χαθήκανε ὅλες
πάλι νὰ παίρνω τὸ βαθύ,
σκοτεινὸ δρόμο μ' εἶδες!

9

Adieu! Adieu! With your heavenly
eyes and with gilly-flowers
at your throat, you left, blonde
hopes of new loves.
Adieu, and you who, turning,
when all have been lost,
you saw me take again
the deep, dark road!

10

Μπρούτζινος γύφτος—τράλαλα!—
τρελὰ πηδάει κεῖ πέρα, χαρούμενος ποὺ ἐδούλευε
τὸν μπροῦτζον ὅλη μέρα
καὶ ποὺ 'χει τὴ γυναῖκα του
χτῆμα του καὶ βασίλειο.
Μπρούτζινος γύφτος—τράλαλα!—
δίνει κλοτσιὰ στὸν ἥλιο!

10

Bronze gypsy—tra-la-la!—
madly he jumps here and there, happy that he worked
the bronze all day
and he has, in his wife,
his land and kingdom.
Bronze gypsy—tra-la-la!—
gives a kick to the sun!

ΤΟ ΦΕΓΓΑΡΑΚΙ ΑΠΟΨΕ...

Τὸ φεγγαράκι ἀπόψε στὸ γιαλὸ
θὰ πέσει, ἕνα βαρὺ μαργαριτάρι.
Κι ἀπάνω μου θὰ παίζει τὸ τρελὸ
τρελὸ φεγγάρι.

Ὅλο θὰ σπάει τὸ κῦμα ρουμπινὶ
στὰ πόδια μου σκορπίζοντας ἀστέρια.
Οἱ παλάμες μου θά 'χουνε γενεῖ
δυὸ περιστέρια·

Θ' ἀνέβουν—ἀσημένια δυὸ πουλιὰ—
μὲ φεγγάρι—δυὸ κοῦπες—θὰ γεμίσουν,
μὲ φεγγάρι τοὺς ὤμους, τὰ μαλλιὰ
θὰ μοῦ ραντίζουν.

Τὸ πέλαγο χρυσάφι ἀναλυτό.
Θὰ βάλω τ' ὄνειρό μου σὲ καΐκι
ν' ἀρμενίσει. Διαμάντι θὰ πατῶ
λαμπρὸ χαλίκι.

Τὸ γύρω φῶς ὡς θᾶν τὴ διαπερνᾷ,
ἡ καρδιά μου βαρὺ μαργαριτάρι.
Καὶ θὰ γελῶ. Καὶ θὲ νὰ κλαίω... Καὶ νά,
νὰ τὸ φεγγάρι!

THE MOON TONIGHT...

The moon tonight will fall
 on the shore, a great pearl.
And above me will be playing
madly the mad moon.

All ruby the wave will break
scattering stars at my feet.
The palms of my hands will be changed,
turned into two doves.

They will rise—two silver birds—
they will fill—two cups—with the moon;
onto my shoulders, my hair, will
spill down the moon's light.

The ocean is molten gold.
I shall set my dream in a boat
to sail away; I shall tread diamond
bright on the shore stones.

The enfolding light shall pierce
my heart, a great pearl.
I shall laugh. Perhaps I shall weep...
There is the moon, there!

MONO

Ἄχ, ὅλα ἔπρεπε νά 'ρθουν καθὼς ἦρθαν!
Οἱ ἐλπίδες καὶ τὰ ρόδα νὰ μαδήσουν.
Βαρκοῦλες νὰ μοῦ φύγουνε τὰ χρόνια,
νὰ φύγουνε, νὰ σβήσουν.

Ἔτσι, ὅπως ἐχωρίζαμε τὰ βράδια,
γιὰ πάντα νὰ χαθοῦνε τόσοι φίλοι.
Τὸν τόπο ποὺ μεγάλωνα παιδάκι
ν' ἀφήσω κάποιο δείλι.

Τὰ ὡραῖα κι ἁπλὰ κορίτσια—ὤ, ἀγαποῦλες!—
ἡ ζωὴ νὰ μοῦ τὰ πάρει, χοροῦ γῦρος.
Ἀκόμη ὁ πόνος, ἄλλοτε ποὺ εὐώδα,
νὰ μὲ βαραίνει στεῖρος.

Ὅλα ἔπρεπε νὰ γίνουν. Μόνο ἡ νύχτα
δὲν ἔπρεπε γλυκιὰ ἔτσι τώρα νά 'ναι,
νὰ παίζουνε τ' ἀστέρια ἐκεῖ σὰν μάτια
καὶ σὰ νὰ μοῦ γελᾶνε.

ONLY

Ah, everything had to come as it came!
That the hopes and the roses fall.
The boats leave me, the years,
that they leave, go out.

Thus, as we used to go our ways in the evenings,
so many friends would be forever lost.
The land where I grew up a child
would be left some twilight.

The simple, lovely girls—oh, loved ones!—
that life should take them from me in the ring-dance of time,
that even now the pain, once so fragrant,
barren, weigh me down.

Everything had to happen. Only the night
need not be so sweet, now, as it is,
that the stars play there like eyes
as if laughing to me.

ΤΕΛΕΥΤΑΙΟ ΤΑΞΙΔΙ

Καλὸ ταξίδι, ἀλαργινὸ καράβι μου, στοῦ ἀπείρου
καὶ στῆς νυχτὸς τὴν ἀγκαλιά, μὲ τὰ χρυσά σου φῶτα!
Νά 'μουν στὴν πλώρη σου ἤθελα, γιὰ νὰ κοιτάζω γύρου
σὲ λιτανεία νὰ περνοῦν τὰ ὀνείρατα τὰ πρῶτα.

Ἡ τρικυμία στὸ πέλαγος καὶ στὴ ζωὴ νὰ παύει,
μακριὰ μαζί σου φεύγοντας πέτρα νὰ ρίχνω πίσω,
νὰ μοῦ λικνίζεις τὴν αἰώνια θλίψη μου, καράβι,
δίχως νὰ ξέρω ποῦ μὲ πᾶς καὶ δίχως νὰ γυρίσω!

FINAL JOURNEY

Bon voyage, my distant ship, in the arms
of infinity and night, with your golden lights!
Might I be at your prow, to look around me
at first dreams, passing in procession.

May the storms of sea and of life cease,
leaving for afar with you, throwing a stone behind,
may you rock my eternal sadness, ship,
knowing not where you take me, and with no return!

ΟΛΟΙ ΜΑΖΙ...

Ὅλοι μαζὶ κινοῦμε, συρφετός,
γυρεύοντας ὁμοιοκαταληξία.
Μιὰ τόσο εὐγενικιὰ φιλοδοξία
ἔγινε τῆς ζωῆς μας ὁ σκοπός.

Ἀλλάζουμε μὲ ἤχους καὶ συλλαβὲς
τὰ αἰσθήματα στὴ χάρτινη καρδιά μας,
δημοσιεύουμε τὰ ποιήματά μας,
γιὰ νὰ τιτλοφορούμεθα ποιητές.

Ἀφήνουμε στὸ ἀγέρι τὰ μαλλιὰ
καὶ τὴ γραβάτα μας. Παίρνουμε πόζα.
Ἀνυπόφορη νομίζουμε πρόζα
τῶν καλῶν ἀνθρώπων τὴ συντροφιά.

Μόνο γιὰ μᾶς ὑπάρχουν τοῦ Θεοῦ
τὰ πλάσματα καί, βέβαια, ὅλη ἡ φύσις.
Στὴ Γῆ γιὰ νὰ στέλνουμε ἀνταποκρίσεις,
ἀνεβήκαμε στ' ἄστρα τ' οὐρανοῦ.

Κι ἂν πειναλέοι γυρνᾶμε ὁλημερίς,
κι ἂν ξενυχτοῦμε κάτου ἀπ' τὰ γεφύρια,
ἐπέσαμε θύματα ἐξιλαστήρια
τοῦ «περιβάλλοντος», τῆς «ἐποχῆς».

ALL TOGETHER...

All together, in a rout,
seeking end-rhyme, we set out:
such a well-bred, fine intention
has become our life's ambition.

By lexical manipulations
we change our paper hearts' emotions;
our poems in the papers show it:
we earn the right to be called 'Poet'.

Free in the wind our long hair flows,
also our ties: we strike a pose.
Prose we judge beyond enduring,
normal people far too boring.

Just for us God made each creature,
and indeed the whole of nature.
Sending reports to depths terrestrial,
we raise ourselves to heights celestial.

What though we spend our days unfed,
under bridges find our bed?
That's our sacrificial fate,
victims of 'Time's Current State'.

ΙΔΑΝΙΚΟΙ ΑΥΤΟΧΕΙΡΕΣ

Γυρίζουν τὸ κλειδὶ στὴν πόρτα, παίρνουν
τὰ παλιά, φυλαγμένα γράμματά τους,
διαβάζουν ἥσυχα, κι ἔπειτα σέρνουν
γιὰ τελευταία φορὰ τὰ βήματά τους.

Ἦταν ἡ ζωή τους, λένε, τραγῳδία.
Θεέ μου, τὸ φρικτὸ γέλιο τῶν ἀνθρώπων,
τὰ δάκρυα, ὁ ἵδρως, ἡ νοσταλγία
τῶν οὐρανῶν, ἡ ἐρημιὰ τῶν τόπων.

Στέκονται στὸ παράθυρο, κοιτᾶνε
τὰ δέντρα, τὰ παιδιά, πέρα τὴ φύση,
τοὺς μαρμαράδες ποὺ σφυροκοπᾶνε,
τὸν ἥλιο ποὺ γιὰ πάντα θέλει δύσει.

Ὅλα τελείωσαν. Τὸ σημείωμα νά το,
σύντομο, ἁπλό, βαθύ, καθὼς ταιριάζει,
ἀδιαφορία, συγχώρηση γεμάτο
γιὰ κεῖνον ποὺ θὰ κλαίει καὶ θὰ διαβάζει.

Βλέπουν τὸν καθρέφτη, βλέπουν τὴν ὥρα,
ρωτοῦν ἂν εἶναι τρέλα τάχα ἢ λάθος,
«ὅλα τελείωσαν» ψιθυρίζουν «τώρα»,
πὼς θ' ἀναβάλουν βέβαιοι κατὰ βάθος.

IDEAL SUICIDES

They turn the key in the door-lock, pick up
their leftover letters.
Calmly they read them, and drag
their feet one last time.

They say their life was a tragedy.
My God, people's terrible laughter;
the tears, the sweat, the yearning
for heaven—the desert of lands.

They stand at the window, look at trees,
the children, and there, over there, nature,
the marbles, beaten with iron hammers,
the sun which is forever setting.

Everything ends. The note? There it is:
short and simple, deep, as it should be,
full of indifference, full of forgiveness
for those who will weep and will weep.

They look in the mirror, look at the time,
ask if it's madness or a mistake.
'All is finished', they whisper, 'now',
certain they will postpone in the end.

Ο ΜΙΧΑΛΙΟΣ

Τὸ Μιχαλιὸ τὸν πήρανε στρατιώτη.
Καμαρωτὰ ξεκίνησε κι ὡραῖα
μὲ τὸ Μαρῆ καὶ μὲ τὸν Παναγιώτη.
Δὲν μπόρεσε νὰ μάθει κἂν τὸ «ἐπ᾽ ὤμου».
Ὅλο ἐμουρμούριζε: «Κὺρ Δεκανέα,
ἄσε με νὰ γυρίσω στὸ χωριό μου».

Τὸν ἄλλο χρόνο, στὸ νοσοκομεῖο,
ἀμίλητος τὸν οὐρανὸ κοιτοῦσε.
Ἐκάρφωνε πέρα, σ᾽ ἕνα σημεῖο,
τὸ βλέμμα του νοσταλγικὸ καὶ πρᾶο,
σὰ νά 'λέγε, σὰ νὰ παρακαλοῦσε:
«Ἀφῆστε με στὸ σπίτι μου νὰ πάω».

Κι ὁ Μιχαλιὸς ἐπέθανε στρατιώτης.
Τὸν ξεπροβόδισαν κάτι φαντάροι,
μαζί τους ὁ Μαρῆς κι ὁ Παναγιώτης.
Ἀπάνω του σκεπάστηκεν ὁ λάκκος,
μὰ τοῦ ἄφησαν ἀπέξω τὸ ποδάρι:
Ἦταν λίγο μακρὺς ὁ φουκαράκος.

MICHALIOS

Michalios was called up for a soldier.
Proudly, handsomely, he set out,
with Maris and Panayiotis.
He couldn't even learn the 'Shoulder arms'.
He kept moaning 'Mr Corporal,
let me go back to my village.'

Next year, in hospital,
speechless, he gazed at the sky:
stuck on one spot, his gaze
gentle and nostalgic,
as if he were saying—begging—
'Let me go home.'

And Michalios died a soldier.
Some recruits saw him off,
among them Maris and Panayiotis.
The grave closed over him,
but they left one foot sticking out:
he was rather tall, the poor sod.

ΩΧΡΑ ΣΠΕΙΡΟΧΑΙΤΗ

Ἦταν ὡραῖα σύνολα τὰ ἐπιστημονικὰ
βιβλία, οἱ αἱματόχαρες εἰκόνες τους, ἡ φίλη
ποὺ ἀμφίβολα κοιτάζοντας ἐγέλα μυστικά,
ὡραῖο κι ὅ,τι μᾶς ἐδίναν τὰ φευγαλέα της χείλη...

Τὸ μέτωπό μας ἔκρουσε τόσο ἁπαλά, μὲ τόση
ἐπιμονή, ποὺ ἀνοίξαμε γιὰ νά 'μπει σὰν κυρία
ἡ Τρέλα στὸ κεφάλι μας, ἔπειτα νὰ κλειδώσει.
Τώρα ἡ ζωή μας γίνεται ξένη, παλιὰ ἱστορία.

Τὸ λογικό, τὰ αἰσθήματά μας εἶναι πολυτέλεια,
βάρος, καὶ τὰ χαρίζουμε τοῦ κάθε συνετοῦ.
Κρατοῦμε τὴν παρόρμηση, τὰ παιδικά μας γέλια,
τὸ ἔνστικτο ν' ἀφηνόμεθα στὸ χέρι τοῦ Θεοῦ.

Μιὰ κωμῳδία ἡ πλάση Του σὰν εἶναι φρικαλέα,
Ἐκεῖνος, ποὺ ἔχει πάντοτε τὴν πρόθεση καλή,
εὐδόκησε στὰ μάτια μας νὰ κατεβάσει αὐλαία
—ὤ, κωμῳδία!—τὸ θάμπωμα, τ' ὄνειρο, τὴν ἀχλύ.

...Κι ἦταν ὡραία ὡς σύνολο ἡ ἀγορασμένη φίλη,
στὸ δείλι αὐτὸ τοῦ μακρινοῦ πέρα χειμῶνος, ὅταν,
γελώντας αἰνιγματικά, μᾶς ἔδινε τὰ χείλη
κι ἔβλεπε τὸ ἐνδεχόμενο, τὴν ἄβυσσο ποὺ ἐρχόταν.

YELLOW SPIROCHETE

They were fine, all together, the scientific books,
their blood-coloured pictures, the friend who,
looking doubtfully, secretly laughed;
fine, too, what her fleeting lips gave us…

It knocked on our forehead so gently, with such patience,
the Madness, that we opened to let it in to our head
like a lady, and then to lock it in.
Now our life becomes a strange, old story.

Our reason, our feelings are luxury,
a burden, and we give them to all who are worthy.
We keep the urge, our childish laughter;
the instinct we leave in the hand of God.

A comedy, His creation, like something frightful:
He, who always has good intentions,
deigned to bring down the curtain before our eyes.
—Oh, comedy!—the dazzle, the dream, the mist.

…And she was altogether fine, the bought friend,
that far distant winter evening when,
laughing enigmatically, she gave us the lips
and saw the consequence; the coming abyss.

ΜΙΚΡΗ ΑΣΥΜΦΩΝΙΑ ΕΙΣ Α ΜΕΙΖΟΝ

Ἄ! κύριε, κύριε Μαλακάση,
ποιὸς θὰ βρεθεῖ νὰ μᾶς δικάσει,
μικρὸν ἐμὲ κι ἐσᾶς μεγάλο
ἴδια τὸν ἕνα καὶ τὸν ἄλλο;

Τοὺς τρόπους, τὸ παράστημά σας,
τὸ θελκτικὸ μειδίαμά σας,
τὸ monocle ποὺ σᾶς βοηθάει
νὰ βλέπετε μόνο στὸ πλάϊ

καὶ μόνο αὐτοὺς νὰ χαιρετᾶτε
ὅσοι μοιάζουν ἀριστοκράται,
τὴν περιποιημένη φάτσα,
τὴν ὑπεροπτικὴ γκριμάτσα

ἀπὸ τὴ μία μεριὰ νὰ βάλει
τῆς ζυγαριᾶς, κι ἀπὸ τὴν ἄλλη
πλάστιγγα νὰ βροντήσω κάτου,
μισητὸ σκήνωμα, θανάτου

ἄθυρμα, συντριμμένο βάζον,
ἐγώ, κύμβαλον ἀλαλάζον.
Ἄ! κύριε, κύριε Μαλακάση,
ποιὸς τελευταῖος θὰ γελάσει;

LITTLE UN-SYMPHONY IN A-MAJOR

Ah, Sir, Mr Malakasi,
who could be found to consider us
—small as I am and great as you are—
one the equal of the other?

Your manners, your bearing,
your charming smile,
the monocle that helps you
see only sideways

and to greet only those
of similar aristocracy,
the attentive face,
the haughty grimace;

to put all this in one balance-pan,
and the other pan come crashing down
under the hateful remains,
the plaything of death,

the shattered vase,
I, soundless cymbal.
Ah, Sir, Mr Malakasi,
Who shall have the last laugh?

ΣΤΑΔΙΟΔΡΟΜΙΑ

Τὴ σάρκα, τὸ αἷμα θὰ βάλω
σὲ σχῆμα βιβλίου μεγάλο.

«Οἱ στίχοι παρέχουν ἐλπίδες»
θὰ γράψουν οἱ ἐφημερίδες.

«Κλεαρέτη Δίπλα-Μαλάμου»
καὶ δίπλα σ' αὐτὸ τ' ὄνομά μου.

Τὴν ψυχὴ καὶ τὸ σῶμα πάλι
στὴ δουλειὰ θὰ δίνω, στὴν πάλη.

Ἀλλά, μὲ τὴ δύση τοῦ ἡλίου,
θὰ πηγαίνω στοῦ Βασιλείου.

Ἐκεῖ θὰ βρίσκω ὅλους τοὺς ἄλλους
λογίους καὶ τοὺς διδασκάλους.

Τὰ λόγια μου θά 'χουν οὐσία,
ἡ σιωπή μου μιὰ σημασία.

Θηρεύοντας πράγματα αἰώνια,
θ' ἀφήσω νὰ φύγουν τὰ χρόνια.

Θὰ φύγουν, καὶ θά 'ναι ἡ καρδιά μου
σὰ ρόδο ποὺ ἐπάτησα χάμου.

CAREER

I shall set my flesh and blood
in a large-format book.

'These verses are promising,'
will be the papers' opinion.

From a well-known critic
and beside it, my own name.

Once again, my body and soul
I shall give to the work, the struggle.

But with the setting of the sun
I shall go down to Vassiliou's.

There I shall find all the other
writers and teachers.

My words shall have substance,
my silence a meaning.

Hunting the eternal,
I shall let the years pass.

They shall pass, and my heart will be
like a rose that I trampled down.

ΠΡΕΒΕΖΑ

Θάνατος εἶναι οἱ κάργες ποὺ χτυπιοῦνται
στοὺς μαύρους τοίχους καὶ τὰ κεραμύδια,
θάνατος οἱ γυναῖκες, ποὺ ἀγαπιοῦνται
καθὼς νὰ καθαρίζουνε κρεμμύδια.

Θάνατος οἱ λεροί, ἀσήμαντοι δρόμοι
μὲ τὰ λαμπρά, μεγάλα ὀνόματά τους,
ὁ ἐλαιῶνας, γύρω ἡ θάλασσα, κι ἀκόμη
ὁ ἥλιος, θάνατος μὲς στοὺς θανάτους.

Θάνατος ὁ ἀστυνόμος ποὺ διπλώνει
γιὰ νὰ ζυγίσῃ μία «ἐλλειπὴ» μερίδα,
θάνατος τὰ ζουμπούλια στὸ μπαλκόνι,
κι ὁ δάσκαλος μὲ τὴν ἐφημερίδα.

Βάσις, Φρουρά, Ἑξηκονταρχία Πρεβέζης.
Τὴν Κυριακὴ θ' ἀκούσουμε τὴν μπάντα.
Ἐπῆρα ἕνα βιβλιάριο Τραπέζης
πρώτη κατάθεσις δραχμαὶ τριάντα.

Περπατώντας ἀργὰ στὴν προκυμαία,
«Ὑπάρχω;» λές, κ' ὕστερα «δὲν ὑπάρχεις!»
Φτάνει τὸ πλοῖο. Ὑψωμένη σημαία.
Ἴσως ἔρχεται ὁ Κύριος Νομάρχης.

PREVEZA

Death is the crows on the tiles
beating against the black walls;
death the women that are loved
as if they're peeling onions.

Death the directionless roads,
dirty, with bright shiny names,
the olive groves and the sea around,
even the sun, death among deaths.

Death the policeman wrapping
to check the grocer's short measure;
death the balcony flowers
and the teacher with his paper.

Garrison, base, petty legion,
Preveza: on Sunday we'll hear the band.
I opened a savings account:
deposited thirty cents.

Slowly walking the quay,
'Do I exist?' you say, then, 'You don't!'
The ferry arrives flying flags.
Perhaps Mr Prefect has come.

Ἄν τουλάχιστον, μέσα στοὺς ἀνθρώπους
αὐτούς, ἕνας ἐπέθαινε ἀπὸ ἀηδία...
Σιωπηλοί, θλιμμένοι, μὲ σεμνοὺς τρόπους,
θὰ διασκεδάζαμε ὅλοι στὴν κηδεία.

If at least among all these people
just one were to die of disgust…
Silently, sad, with respect,
we would rejoice at his grave.

Selected Prose

ΕΝΑΣ ΠΡΑΚΤΙΚΟΣ ΘΑΝΑΤΟΣ

Δὲν ξέρω τί φοροῦσε στὸ κεφάλι. Τὰ ροῦχα της δὲν εἶχαν οὔτε σχῆμα οὔτε χρῶμα. Ἐμπῆκε στὸ γραφεῖο κρατώντας στὴν ἀγκαλιὰ δυὸ παιδιὰ καὶ σέρνοντας τέσσερα. Καθένα ἔκλαιγε ἢ ἐφώναζε μὲ ἰδιαίτερο τρόπο. Ἄλλο τραβοῦσε τὸ φουστάνι της, ἄλλο τὰ μαλλιά της. Ἕνα ἀγόρι ὡς τριῶν χρονῶν ἔτρεμε μὲ κάτι παράξενα ἀναφιλητά, χωρὶς νὰ κλαίει. Ὅλα μαζὶ—φριχτὴ συμφωνία—ἐκοίταζαν τὴ μητέρα τους ὅπως οἱ μουσικοὶ τὸ μαέστρο. Αὐτὴ ὅμως εἶχε ξεχάσει τὴν παρτιτούρα της σ' ἕνα κομψὸ γραφειάκι ἀπὸ acajou.

Στάθηκε μπροστά μας μὲ ὀρθάνοιχτα μάτια. Κάτι σὰν ψεύτικο γέλιο, μιὰ γκριμάτσα οἴκτου πρὸς τὸν ἑαυτό της, ἐξηγοῦσε τὰ λόγια της. Ἦταν Ἀρμένισσα. Ὁ ἄντρας της ἐπέθανε σ' ἕνα χωριό, κ' ἦρθε ἀπὸ κεῖ ζητώντας ψωμὶ γιὰ τὰ παιδιά της. Τώρα παρακαλοῦσε νὰ στεγασθεῖ. Κάποιος ποὺ ἤξερε τὴ γλῶσσα της τῆς εἶπε ὅτι δὲν ὑπῆρχε πουθενὰ θέσις. Καὶ καθὼς δὲν ἤθελε νὰ καταλάβει, τὴν ἔβγαλαν ἔξω στὸ διάδρομο. Ἔμεινε ξαπλωμένη μὲ τὰ παιδιά της ὡς τὸ μεσημέρι. Τὴν ἄλλη μέρα, ἡ ἴδια ἱστορία. Ἦρθε πολλὲς φορὲς ἀκόμη.

Ἐπιτέλους τὴν ἔριξαν σὲ μία ἀποθήκη. Τριάντα οἰκογένειες προσφύγων ποὺ ἔμεναν ἐκεῖ μέσα εἶχαν χωρίσει τὰ νοικοκυριά τους πρόχειρα, μὲ φανταστικοὺς τοίχους. Μπόγοι, κασέλες, κουβέρτες ἁπλωμένες, ξύλα βαλμένα

AN OPPORTUNE DEATH

I don't know what she wore on her head. Her clothes had neither form nor colour. She came into the office with two children in her arms and dragging four more, all of them crying or shouting. One tugged at her skirt, another at her hair. One boy of about three shook with a strange sobbing, without actually crying. All together they watched their mother like musicians the conductor; a frightful symphony. She, however, had left the score on some elegant cashew-wood desk.

She stood wide-eyed before us. Something like a forced laugh, a piteous grimace, was explained by what she said: she was Armenian, her husband had died in some village, and she'd come from there seeking bread for her children. Now, she was begging for shelter. Someone who knew her language told her there wasn't any room, and since she didn't want to understand, they put her out in the corridor. She lay down there with her children until the afternoon. The next day, the same story; she came again many times.

Finally, they shoved her into a storehouse. Thirty refugee families already living there had divided it up into separate households with fantastic improvised walls: bundles, crates, strung-up blankets, bits of wood set in rows, formed little squares; the pugnacious

στὴ γραμμή, ἐσχημάτιζαν τετράγωνα, τὰ μαχητικὰ τετράγωνα τῆς τελευταίας ἀμύνης. Σ' αὐτὲς τὶς φωλιὲς ἀκινητοῦσαν ἢ ἐσάλευαν πένθιμα σκιὲς ἀνθρώπων. Τρεῖς τρεῖς, πέντε πέντε, σκορπισμένοι ἀνάμεσα σὲ ρυπαρὰ ροῦχα καὶ ὑπολείμματα ἐπίπλων, ἦταν σὰ νὰ ψιθύριζαν παραμύθια ἢ νὰ προσπαθοῦσαν σιγὰ ν' ἀποτινάξουν τὸ σκοτάδι.

Τώρα ἡ ἀποθήκη φωτίζεται ἀπὸ ἕνα κερί. Κάποιο δέμα τυλιγμένο μὲ καθαρὸ ἄσπρο πανὶ ἔχει τοποθετηθεῖ προσεκτικά, κάθετα πρὸς τὸν τοῖχο, χάμου. Εἶναι τὸ μικρότερο ἀπὸ τὰ ἔξι παιδιὰ τῆς Ἀρμένισσας, ποὺ πέθανε λίγες ὥρες μετὰ τὴν ἐγκατάστασή τους. Τ' ἀδέλφια του παίζουν ἔξω στὸν ἥλιο. Ἡ μητέρα, ξαλαφρωμένη, παραστέκει γιὰ τελευταία φορὰ τὸ μωρό της. Οἱ ἄλλες γυναῖκες τὴ μακαρίζουν, γιατί θὰ μπορέσει ἀπὸ αὔριο νὰ πιάσει δουλειά. Εἶναι σχεδὸν εὐτυχής. Καὶ ὁ νεκρὸς ἀκόμη περιμένει μὲ τόση ἀξιοπρέπεια...

boundaries of last defence. In these nests, sorry shades of humanity stirred or lay still. Groups of three, four or five, amongst filthy rags and the remains of furniture, seemed to whisper fairytales, or try weakly to ward off the darkness.

Now, the storehouse was lit by a candle: some bundle, wrapped in a clean white cloth, had been laid carefully down low against the wall. It was the smallest of the Armenian woman's six children, and it had died a few hours after they'd found their place here. Its brothers and sisters were playing outside in the sunshine. The mother, relieved now of her burden, had held her baby for the last time. The other women envied her: tomorrow she'd be able to look for work. She's almost lucky. And the dead child, so dignified, waits…

ΤΟ ΚΑΥΚΑΛΟ

Οἱ ἄνθρωποι νομίζουνε πὼς τὰ ξέρουν ὅλα. Ἔτσι κανένας δὲ θά 'θελε νὰ ὑποθέσει πὼς ἕνα καύκαλο μέσα στὴν ὀστεοθήκη του εἶναι κάτι παραπάνω ἀπὸ ὅ,τι πιστεύεται κοινά. Γι' αὐτὸ δὲν ἔτρεμε καθόλου τὸ χέρι τοῦ παράξενου ποιητῆ ὅταν ἦρθε μία μέρα νὰ ταράξει τὸν ὕπνο τῶν αἰώνων ποὺ κοιμόμουν μέσα στὸ μαῦρο μου κασονάκι, ὄξω ἀπὸ τὴν ἐκκλησία τοῦ νεκροταφείου. Τὶς δυὸ μικρὲς σπηλιὲς στὴ βάση τοῦ μετώπου μου —στὴ ζωὴ τ' ὄνομά τους ἦταν γλυκὸ σὰν τὸ φῶς— τὶς γιόμιζε ἡ νύχτα τοῦ ἀσυνείδητου. Κάποια ἀράχνη ἐσάλευε ἀπάνω στὸ μηλίγγι μου κ' εἶχε γίνει τὸ ὄνειρό μου. Ξυπνώντας ἔξαφνα, ἔνοιωσα νὰ μὲ σηκώνουν. Σίγουρα θὰ ἦρθε ἡ ὥρα τοῦ χωνευτηρίου, ἐσκέφτηκα. Μὲ τὸ δίκιο τους θὰ κουράστηκαν οἱ δικοί μου νὰ πληρώνουν τόσα χρόνια τώρα τὸ μισὸ νοῖκι ποὺ ἐξασφάλιζε τὴ θέση μου στὴν αὐλὴ τῆς ἐκκλησίας. Ἀλλὰ δὲν ἦταν αὐτό. Μ' ἐτύλιξαν σὲ μίαν ἐφημερίδα, κ' ὕστερα ἀπὸ λίγην ὥρα ἐβρέθηκα στὸ τραπέζι τῆς μελέτης τοῦ ποιητῆ μου, ἀπάνω σ' ἕνα βιβλίο ποὺ ἔτυχε νά 'ναι κάτι εὔθυμα τραγούδια ἀγάπης.

Στὴν ἀρχὴ μ' ἄφησαν ἥσυχο νὰ κοιτάζω ὅ,τι μποροῦσε νὰ χωρέσει στὸ στενό του κύκλο τὸ βλέμμα μου, ποὺ δὲν ἦταν βέβαια βολετὸ νὰ τὸ διευθύνω ὅπου ἤθελα. Ἀντίκρυ μου ἄσπριζε τὸ κρεβάτι. Οἱ θύμησές

THE SKULL

People think they know everything. So no one wants to think that a skull in an ossuary is anything more than it's commonly supposed to be. That's why the hand of the strange poet didn't tremble at all when he came one day to disturb my eternal sleep in my black box outside the cemetery church.

The two little caves at the base of my forehead—in life, their name was as sweet as light—the night of unconsciousness had filled them. Some spider had crawled across my temple and become my dream. Waking up suddenly, I felt they were raising me. Surely the time for the ossuary has come, I thought.[1] My people will quite rightly be fed up with paying, for so many years now, the little rent that ensures my place in the churchyard. But that wasn't it. They wrapped me up in newspaper, and in a little while I found myself on my poet's study table, on top of a book that happened to be one of jolly love-songs.

At first they left me in peace, to look at whatever could be held in the narrow circle of my gaze, which of

---

[1] It is the custom in Greece to disinter the body after a few years and place the bones in an ossuary.

μου ὁλοένα ἐζωήρευαν μὲ τὸ νὰ τὸ βλέπω. Τώρα θυμόμουν καθαρὰ ἕνα κρεβάτι. Δὲν ἦταν τὸ κρεβάτι τῆς τελευταίας μου ἀρρώστειας. Γιατί τὸ ξεκουραστικὸ κρεβάτι τοῦ θανάτου δὲν τὸ θυμᾶται ἕνα καύκαλο σὰν ἐμένα παρὰ μόνο γιὰ νὰ νοσταλγήσει τὴ ζωή. Θυμόμουν, ὅμως, καθαρὰ ἕνα κρεβάτι. Ὕστερα ἐπέρασε θαμπὸ ἀπὸ τὴ μνήμη μου κάτι ἄλλο... Δὲν μπόρεσα νὰ ξεχωρίσω τί. Πάει τόσος καιρὸς ἀπὸ τότε...

Ἐκοίταζα τὸ ἡμερολόγιο στὸν τοῖχο γιὰ νὰ ἰδῶ πόσα χρόνια ἐβάστηξε ὁ ὕπνος μου, ὅταν ἔνιωσα ἀπὸ τὸ θόρυβο πὼς κάποιος ἐμπῆκε στὴν κάμαρα. Ἦταν ἕνας φίλος τοῦ ἀπαγωγέα μου. Ἦρθε καὶ στάθηκε μπροστά μου. Ὁ ποιητὴς μ' ἔδειξε λέγοντας: «Νὰ σοῦ συστήσω τὸν κύριο...», κ' εἶπε τ' ὄνομά μου, ποὺ τό 'χε διαβάσει στὴν ὀστεοθήκη. Ὁ ἄλλος ὑποκλίθηκε χωρικά, ἔβγαλε τὸ καπέλο του καὶ μοῦ τὸ φόρεσε. Ἄναψε κ' ἕνα τσιγάρο καὶ τὸ σφήνωσε στὰ δόντια μου. Ὕστερα ἀρχίσανε νὰ γελᾶνε. Ἐγὼ τοὺς ἐκοίταζα σοβαρά, ὅπως ταιριάζει, σ' ὅσους ἔζησαν τὴ ζωή, νὰ κοιτοῦνε αὐτοὺς ποὺ θὰ τὴ ζήσουν. Δὲ μὲ πείραζε καθόλου ἕνα τέτοιο φέρσιμο, μόνε συλλογιζόμουνα τί ἀπλοϊκοὶ πού 'ναι οἱ ἄνθρωποι νὰ νομίζουνε πὼς τὰ ξέρουν ὅλα καὶ νὰ μὴ θέλουνε ποτὲ νὰ παραδεχτοῦνε πὼς ἕνα καύκαλο μπορεῖ νά 'ναι κάτι παραπάνω ἀπὸ ὅ,τι πιστεύεται κοινά.

Δυὸ ὁλόκληρες ὧρες ἀναγκάστηκα νὰ τοὺς ἀκούω. Τὰ λόγια τους θὰ μοῦ 'φέρναν πικρὸ τὸ χαμόγελο στὰ χείλη. Μιλούσανε γιὰ τὶς γυναῖκες τους, γιὰ τὰ βιβλία τους, γιὰ κάθε τί, σὰ νὰ μὴν ἦταν τὸ κρανίο ἑνὸς ἀν-

course it wasn't convenient for me to direct wherever I wished. Opposite me was the whiteness of the bed. My memories came to life all at once when I saw it. Now, I clearly remembered a bed. It wasn't the bed of my final illness, because that bed of repose, of death, is not one a skull like me remembers, except out of nostalgia for life. And I didn't feel nostalgia for life. Nevertheless, I clearly remembered a bed. Then something else passed dimly across my memory... I couldn't make out what it was. So much time had passed since then...

I was looking at the calendar on the wall to see how many years my sleep had lasted when I realized from the sound that someone had come into the room. It was a friend of my abductor. He came and stood in front of me. The poet indicated toward me, saying, 'May I introduce Mr...' and added my name, which he'd read on the ossuary. The other bowed boorishly, took off his hat and put it on me. He lit a cigarette and wedged it between my teeth. Then they started to laugh. I looked at them seriously, as befits one who has lived his life when he looks at those who will live it. Such behaviour didn't trouble me; I just reflected how naïve people were to think that they knew everything and would never be willing to accept that a skull might be something more than is commonly thought.

I was obliged to listen to them for two hours. Their words would have brought a bitter smile to my lips. They talked about their wives, about their books, about

θρώπου ὅμοιου μ' αὐτοὺς ἡ μπάλα ἐκείνη τῆς φρίκης ποὺ τὴ ἤξεραν τόσο κοντά τους.

Ἔφύγανε.

Ἀργά, μετὰ τὰ μεσάνυχτα, ἐγύρισε μονάχος ὁ ποιητής. Δὲν ξέρω γιατί ἔνιωσα κάτι σὰν ἕνα αἴσθημα ὑπεροχῆς νὰ μὲ κυριεύει. Καθὼς ἄναβε ἡ λάμπα, τὸ χέρι του δὲν ἦταν ὅμοια σταθερὸ ὅπως ὅταν ἄνοιγε τὸ μαῦρο μου κουτί, στὸ νεκροταφεῖο. Τὸ φῶς, πέφτοντας λοξὰ ἀπάνω μου, μοῦ 'δωσε μίαν ὄψη παράξενα ζωντανή. Τὸ κατάλαβα ἀπὸ τὴν ἔκφραση τοῦ φίλου μου αὐτό. Μὲ πῆρε στὰ χέρι του. Ἄνοιξε τὸ παράθυρο. Θὰ μὲ πετοῦσε στὸ δρόμο, ἄν δὲν ἐκάρφωνα πιὸ μαῦρο καὶ πιὸ βαθὺ τὸ βλέμμα μου στὸ μεταξὺ τῶν ματιῶν του. Μ' ἄφησε στὸ πεζούλι τοῦ παραθύρου κ' ἔκλεισε. Ὅλη τὴ νύχτα τὸν ἄκουγα νὰ στριφογυρίζει στὸ κρεβάτι. Ἄν ἐκοιμήθηκε, θά 'κάνε πολὺ ταραγμένο ὕπνο.

Τὸ πρωὶ βρέθηκα μέσα στὴν ὀστεοθήκη μου. Χωρὶς ἄλλο θὰ μ' ἔφερε στὴ θέση μου ὁ ἴδιος ἐκεῖνος τύπος μὲ τὰ παράξενα γοῦστα. Τώρα ἀκουμπῶ τὸ σαγόνι μου στοχαστικὰ στὸ κόκκαλο τοῦ χεριοῦ καὶ σκέφτομαι τὴν περιπέτειά μου. Μοῦ φαίνεται πὼς βλέπω ἀκόμα τὸ βιβλίο μὲ τὰ εὔθυμα ἐρωτικὰ τραγούδια καὶ τὸ ἡμερολόγιο μὲ τὴν τραγικὰ προχωρημένη ἡμερομηνία. Περσότερο ὅμως συλλογιέμαι τὸ κρεβάτι. Τὸ κρεβάτι μ' ἔκαμε νὰ μισοθυμηθῶ μιὰ μικρὴ ἱστορία ποὺ ἐνόμιζα πὼς εἶχα κατορθώσει νὰ ξεχάσω ὁλότελα.

everything, just as if the frightful sphere beside them were not the skull of a person like themselves.

They left.

Late, after midnight, the poet returned alone. I don't know why I felt myself overcome by a feeling of superiority. As he lit the lamp, his hand wasn't as steady as it had been when he opened my black box at the cemetery. The light, glancing sideways on me, gave me a strange appearance of life, as I realized from the expression of this friend of mine. He took me in his hands. He opened the window. He would have thrown me into the street, had I not fixed my gaze, darker and deeper, between his eyes. He left me on the ledge and closed the window. All night I heard him tossing and turning in bed. If he slept at all, it would have been a very troubled sleep.

In the morning, I found myself back in my ossuary. Without doubt, this chap with strange tastes must have put me back in my place. Now I rest my chin reflectively on the bones of my hand and think about my adventure. It seems to me I can still see the book with the merry erotic songs, and the calendar with its tragically advanced date. Most of all, though, I think about the bed. The bed made me half remember a little story which I thought I'd succeeded in completely forgetting.

Ο ΚΗΠΟΣ ΤΗΣ ΑΧΑΡΙΣΤΙΑΣ

Θὰ καλλιεργήσω τὸ ὡραιότερο ἄνθος. Στὶς καρδιὲς τῶν ἀνθρώπων θὰ φυτέψω τὴν Ἀχαριστία. Εὐνοϊκοὶ εἶναι οἱ καιροί, κατάλληλος ὁ τόπος. Ὁ ἄνεμος τσακίζει τὰ δέντρα. Στὴ νοσηρὴ ἀτμόσφαιρα ὀρθώνονται φίδια. Οἱ ἐγκέφαλοι, ἐργαστήρια κιβδηλοποιῶν. Τερατώδη νήπια τὰ ἔργα, ὑπάρχουν στὶς γυάλες. Καὶ μέσα σὲ δάσος ἀπὸ μάσκες, ζήτησε νὰ ζήσεις. Ἐγὼ θὰ καλλιεργήσω τὴν Ἀχαριστία.

Ὅταν ἔρθει ἡ τελευταία ἄνοιξις, ὁ κῆπος μου θά 'ναι γεμάτος ἀπὸ θεσπέσια δείγματα τοῦ εἴδους. Τὰ σεληνοφώτιστα βράδια, μονάχος θὰ περπατῶ στοὺς καμπυλωτοὺς δρόμους, μετρώντας αὐτὰ τὰ λουλούδια. Πλησιάζοντας μὲ κλειστὰ μάτια τὴ βελούδινη, σκοτεινὴ στεφάνη τους, θὰ νιώθω στὸ πρόσωπο τοὺς αἰχμηρούς των στημόνες καὶ θ' ἀναπνέω τ' ἄρωμά τους.

Οἱ ὧρες θὰ περνοῦν, θὰ γυρίζουν τ' ἄστρα, καὶ οἱ αὖρες θὰ πνέουν, ἀλλὰ ἐγώ, γέρνοντας ὁλοένα περσότερο, θὰ θυμᾶμαι.

Θὰ θυμᾶμαι τὶς σφιγμένες γροθιές, τὰ παραπλανητικὰ χαμόγελα καὶ τὴν προδοτικὴ ἀδιαφορία.

Θὰ μένω ἀκίνητος ἡμέρες καὶ χρόνια, χωρὶς νὰ σκέπτομαι, χωρὶς νὰ βλέπω, χωρὶς νὰ ἐκφράζω τίποτε ἄλλο. Θὰ εἶμαι ὁλόκληρος μία πικρὴ ἀνάμνησις, ἕνα ἄγαλμα ποὺ γύρω του θὰ μεγαλώνουν τροπικὰ φυτά,

THE GARDEN OF INGRATITUDE

I shall cultivate the loveliest flower. In the hearts of men I shall plant Ingratitude. The times are propitious, the place appropriate. The wind tears down the trees. Snakes rise up in the morbid air. Brains are workshops of forgery. The preserving jars hold monstrous infants, and, though it be in a forest of disguises, you should seek to live. I shall cultivate Ingratitude.

When the final spring comes, my garden will be full of superb specimens of that variety. On moonlit nights I shall walk alone on the winding paths, counting these flowers. Approaching, eyes closed, their dark, velvet wreath, I shall feel on my face the pricks of their stamens, and I shall breathe their scent.

The hours shall pass, the stars will revolve, and the terraces will breathe, but I, leaning more and more, shall remember.

I shall remember the clenched fists, the deceitful smiles and the treacherous indifference.

I shall remain motionless for days and years, without thinking, without seeing, without expressing anything else. I shall be entirely a bitter memory, a statue round which tropical plants will grow, they will become denser, twisted together, they will conquer the earth and the air. Slowly, their stems will squeeze round my

θὰ πυκνώνουν, θὰ μπερδεύονται μεταξύ τους, θὰ κερδίζουν τὴ γῆ καὶ τὸν ἀέρα. Σιγὰ σιγὰ οἱ κλῶνοι τους θὰ περισφίγγουν τὸ λαιμό μου, θὰ πλέκονται στὰ μαλλιά μου, θὰ μὲ τυλίγουν μὲ ἀνθρώπινη περίσκεψη.

Κάτου ἀπὸ τὴ σταθερή τους ὤθηση, θὰ βυθίζομαι στὸ χῶμα.

Καὶ ὁ κῆπος μου θὰ εἶναι ὁ κῆπος τῆς Ἀγάπης.

throat, they will tangle in my hair, they will wrap me in human wariness.

    Beneath their continual pressure I shall sink into the earth.

    And my garden will be the garden of Love.

Η ΑΠΟΧΑΙΡΕΤΙΣΤΗΡΙΑ ΕΠΙΣΤΟΛΗ

21η Ιουλίου 1928
Ο ποιητής αυτοκτονεί. Η τελευταία επιστολή του βρέθηκε στην τσέπη του παλτού του.

Εἶναι καιρὸς νὰ φανερώσω τὴν τραγῳδία μου. Τὸ μεγαλύτερό μου ἐλάττωμα στάθηκε ἡ ἀχαλίνωτη περιέργειά μου, ἡ νοσηρὴ φαντασία καὶ ἡ προσπάθειά μου νὰ πληροφορηθῶ γιὰ ὅλες τὶς συγκινήσεις, χωρὶς τὶς περσότερες, νὰ μπορῶ νὰ τὶς αἰσθανθῶ. Τὴ χυδαία ὅμως πράξη ποὺ μοῦ ἀποδίδεται τὴ μισῶ. Ἐζήτησα μόνο τὴν ἰδεατὴ ἀτμόσφαιρά της, τὴν ἔσχατη πικρία. Οὔτε εἶμαι ὁ κατάλληλος ἄνθρωπος γιὰ τὸ ἐπάγγελμα ἐκεῖνο. Ὁλόκληρο τὸ παρελθόν μου πείθει γι' αὐτό. Κάθε πραγματικότης μοῦ ἦταν ἀποκρουστική.

Εἶχα τὸν ἴλιγγο τοῦ κινδύνου. Καὶ τὸν κίνδυνο ποὺ ἦρθε τὸν δέχομαι μὲ πρόθυμη καρδιά. Πληρώνω γιὰ ὅσους, καθὼς ἐγώ, δὲν ἔβλεπαν κανένα ἰδανικὸ στὴ ζωή τους, ἔμειναν πάντα ἔρμαια τῶν δισταγμῶν τους, ἢ ἐθεώρησαν τὴν ὕπαρξή τους παιχνίδι χωρὶς οὐσία. Τοὺς βλέπω νὰ ἔρχονται ὁλοένα περισσότεροι μαζὶ μὲ τοὺς αἰῶνες. Σ' αὐτοὺς ἀπευθύνομαι.

Ἀφοῦ ἐδοκίμασα ὅλες τὶς χαρές!!! εἶμαι ἕτοιμος γιὰ ἕναν ἀτιμωτικὸ θάνατο. Λυποῦμαι τοὺς δυστυχισμέ-

THE LAST LETTER

21st of July 1928
The poet puts an end to his life. His last letter was found in the pocket of his jacket.

It's time to reveal my tragedy. My greatest fault was always my unbridled curiosity, my morbid fantasy, my attempt to investigate all the emotions, without being able to feel most of them. I hate the vulgar deed that has been attributed to me. I sought only its ideal atmosphere, its ultimate bitterness; nor am I the appropriate person for that profession. All my past is evidence of that. All possible eventualities were repulsive to me.

I felt the dizziness of danger. And when that danger came, I accepted it with an eager heart. I pay for those who, like me, saw nothing ideal in their lives, who were always prey to doubts, and considered their existence an empty game. As the ages pass, I see more and more such coming. To these I appeal.

Yet I tasted all the joys!!! I'm ready now for a dishonourable death. I'm sorry for my unfortunate parents, I'm sorry for my brother and sister. But I leave with my head held high. I was sick.

νους γονεῖς μου, λυποῦμαι τὰ ἀδέλφια μου. Ἀλλὰ φεύγω μὲ τὸ μέτωπο ψηλά. Ἤμουν ἄρρωστος.

Σᾶς παρακαλῶ νὰ τηλεγραφήσετε, γιὰ νὰ προδιαθέσῃ τὴν οἰκογένειά μου, στὸ θεῖο μου Δημοσθένη Καρυωτάκη, ὁδὸς Μονῆς Προδρόμου, πάροδος Ἀριστοτέλους, Ἀθήνας.

Κ.Γ.Κ.

[Υ.Γ.] Καὶ γιὰ ν᾽ ἀλλάξουμε τόνο. Συμβουλεύω ὅσους ξέρουν κολύμπι νὰ μὴν ἐπιχειρήσουνε ποτὲ νὰ αὐτοκτονήσουν διὰ θαλάσσης. Ὅλη νύχτα ἀπόψε ἐπὶ δέκα ὧρες, ἐδερνόμουν μὲ τὰ κύματα. Ἤπια ἄφθονο νερό, ἀλλὰ κάθε τόσο, χωρὶς νὰ καταλάβω πῶς, τὸ στόμα μου ἀνέβαινε στὴν ἐπιφάνεια. Ὡρισμένως, κάποτε, ὅταν μοῦ δοθεῖ ἡ εὐκαιρία, θὰ γράψω τὶς ἐντυπώσεις ἑνὸς πνιγμένου.

Please send a telegram to my uncle Demosthenes Karyotakis, Monis Prodromou street, off Aristotelous street, Athens, asking him to break the news to my family.

K.G.K.

P.S. And to change the tone: I advise those who know how to swim never to employ the sea as a means of suicide. All last night, for ten hours, I was beaten by the waves. I swallowed copious amounts of water, but without my knowing how, every so often my body came back up to the surface. Some time, when I get the chance, I shall write the impressions of someone drowning.

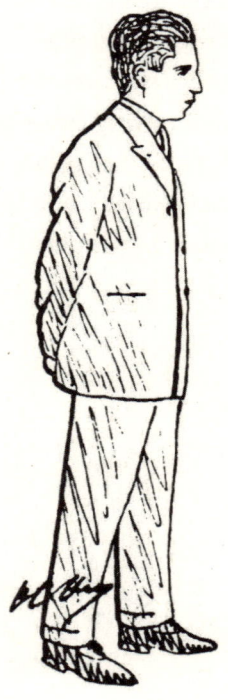

Karyotakis' drawing of himself.

Chronology

1896   Kostas Karyotakis is born on the 30th of October; the second of three children of Yorgos and Katerina Karyotakis.

1909   The family moves to Athens; one of many moves (his father was a public-works inspector).

1912   First poems are published in periodicals such as *Parnassos*.

1913   Finishes secondary education and, in September, enrolls in the Athens Law School.

1917   Graduates from Athens Law School, graded 'very good'.

1918   Enrolls in the School of Philosophy at Athens University, postponing his military service.

1919   Sets up legal practice in Athens, but unsuccessfully. In February, his first collection of poems *The Suffering of Man and of Objects* is published. In October, he is appointed as ministerial secretary in the district government of Thessaloniki. Starts,

with other writers, the satirical magazine *The Leg*, but it is closed down by the police after six issues.

1920   Excused from military service on health grounds. Transfers to the district government of Arta. In August, writes a one-act play, *The Invalid*. Transfers to the district government of Arta.

1921   In September, publication of second collection of poems, *Nepenthe*. In October, he is transferred to the district government of the Cyclades, and in December, to that of Attica. (These frequent transfers, continuing all his life, were certainly caused in part by his finding his work uncongenial.)

1922   Several poems published in various periodicals. Begins love affair with the poet Maria Polydouri, a work colleague. At about the same time he is diagnosed with syphilis, but in October she writes to him proposing that they live together without having children.

1923   Writes the first version of his poem 'Yellow Spirochete', about his diagnosis with syphilis.

1924   In October, Maria Polydouri is engaged to Yorgos Aristotelis.

1925   Polidouri breaks off their engagement and goes to Paris. She falls ill with tuberculosis.

1927   His third collection *Elegies and Satires* is rejected by one publisher, but Karyotakis tells a close friend, 'I have nothing better than this to give' and finally partly underwrites its release from another publisher in July. Writes to the poet Miltiades

Malakasis, once his friend, to ask forgiveness for the poem in the collection *Little Unsymphony in A-Major*, in which Karyotakis satirizes Malakasi. In December, his pay is reduced because he has revealed damaging facts about his state employers to an anti-government newspaper.

1928 In April, Polydouri returns to Athens and is hospitalized. Meanwhile, Karyotakis takes leave and visits Paris. In June, he is transferred to the Prefecture of Preveza, where he works as a lawyer controlling land donations from the state to refugees from the 1922 Smyrna catastrophe. Writes perhaps his best-known and bitterly satirical poem entitled simply 'Preveza'. On 21 July, he shoots himself through the heart on a beach near Preveza, following a night spent trying to drown himself. A suicide letter is found in his pocket.

Index of Greek Titles

Δέντρο	32
Δον Κιχώτες	22
Ένας πρακτικός θάνατος	78
Η αποχαιρετιστήρια επιστολή	92
Ιδανικοί αυτόχειρες	62
Μικρή ασυμφωνία εις Α μείζον	68
Μόνο	56
Μπαλάντα στους άδοξους ποιητές των αιώνων	28
Νύχτα	18
Ο κήπος της αχαριστίας	88
Ο Μιχαλιός	64
Όλοι μαζί...	60
Πολύμνια	24
Πρέβεζα	72
Σταδιοδρομία	70
Στροφές 1–10	34
Τελευταίο ταξίδι	58
Το καύκαλο	82
Το φεγγαράκι απόψε...	54
Ωχρά σπειροχαίτη	66

MODERN GREEK CLASSICS

The MODERN GREEK CLASSICS series highlights the most significant Greek writers, poets, and works of literature since the nineteenth century in translation—a tour of different forms, authors and periods of modern Greek literature.

aiorabooks.com

C.P. CAVAFY
Selected Poems
BILINGUAL EDITION
Translated by David Connolly

Cavafy is by far the most translated and well-known Greek poet internationally. Whether his subject matter is historical, philosophical or sensual, Cavafy's unique poetic voice is always recognizable by its ironical, suave, witty and world-weary tones.

STRATIS DOUKAS
A Prisoner of War's Story
Translated by Petro Alexiou
With an Afterword by Dimitris Tziovas

A classic tale of survival in a time of nationalist conflict, *A Prisoner of War's Story* is a beautifully crafted and pithy narrative. Affirming the common humanity of peoples, it earns its place among Europe's finest anti-war literature of the post-WWI period.

ODYSSEUS ELYTIS   1979 NOBEL PRIZE FOR LITERATURE
In the Name of Luminosity and Transparency
With an Introduction by Dimitris Daskalopoulos

The poetry of Odysseus Elytis owes as much to the ancients and Byzantium as to the surrealists of the 1930s, bringing romantic modernism and structural experimentation to Greece. Collected here are the two speeches Elytis gave on his acceptance of the 1979 Nobel Prize for Literature.

NIKOS ENGONOPOULOS
Cafés and Comets After Midnight and Other Poems
BILINGUAL EDITION
Translated by David Connolly

Derided for his innovative and, at the time, often incomprehensible modernist experiments, Engonopoulos is today regarded as one of the most original artists of his generation. In both his painting and poetry, he created a peculiarly Greek surrealism, a blending of the Dionysian and Apollonian.

M. KARAGATSIS
Junkermann
Translated by Patricia Barbeito

A modernist, picaresque epic, set in the interwar period, *Junkermann* recounts the life and times of a hedonistic Finnish nobleman with a checkered past who serves as a Cossack guard in the Czar's army, flees the Bolshevik revolution, and seeks his fortune as he finally settles in Greece..

M. KARAGATSIS
The Great Chimera
Translated by Patricia Barbeito

A psychological portrait of a young French woman, Marina, who marries a sailor and moves to the island of Syros. Her fate grows entwined with that of the boats and when economic downturn arrives, it brings passion, life and death in its wake.

KOSTAS KARYOTAKIS
Ballad for the Unsung Poets of the Ages
BILINGUAL EDITION

Translated by Simon Darragh

Karyotakis is the poet most emblematic of the turbulent interwar period in Greece. His poetry is often pessimistic and bitingly satirical. His writing combines reverie with sarcasm, a stifling sense of everyday reality with poignant irony. This is verse that is both piercing and resonant.

ANDREAS LASKARATOS
Reflections
BILINGUAL EDITION

Translated by Simon Darragh

Andreas Laskaratos was a writer and poet, a social thinker and, in many ways, a controversialist. His *Reflections* sets out, in a series of calm, clear and pithy aphorisms, his uncompromising and finely reasoned beliefs on morality, justice, personal conduct, power, tradition, religion and government.

MARGARITA LIBERAKI
The Other Alexander
Translated by Willis Barnstone and Elli Tzalopoulou Barnstone

A tyrannical father leads a double life; he has two families and gives the same first names to both sets of children. The half-siblings meet, love, hate, and betray one another. Hailed by Albert Camus as "true poetry," Liberaki's sharp, riveting prose consolidates her place in European literature.

ALEXANDROS PAPADIAMANDIS
Fey Folk
Translated by David Connolly

Alexandros Papadiamandis holds a special place in the history of Modern Greek letters, but also in the heart of the ordinary reader. *Fey Folk* follows the humble lives of quaint, simple-hearted folk living in accordance with centuries-old traditions, described here with both reverence and humour.

ALEXANDROS RANGAVIS
The Notary
Translated by Simon Darragh

A mystery set on the island of Cephalonia, this classic work of Rangavis is an iconic tale of suspense and intrigue, love and murder. *The Notary* is Modern Greek literature's contribution to the tradition of early crime fiction, alongside E.T.A. Hoffman, Edgar Allan Poe and Wilkie Collins.

EMMANUEL ROÏDES
Pope Joan
Translated by David Connolly

This satirical novel, a masterpiece of modern Greek literature, retells the legend of a female pope as a disguised criticism of the Orthodox Church of the nineteenth century. It was a bestseller across Europe at its time and the controversy it provoked led to the swift excommunication of its author.

ANTONIS SAMARAKIS
The Flaw
Translated by Simon Darragh

A man is seized from his afternoon drink at the Cafe Sport by two agents of the Regime by car toward Special Branch Headquarters, and the interrogation that undoubtedly awaits him there. Part thriller and part political satire, *The Flaw* has been translated into more than thirty languages.

DIONYSIS SAVVOPOULOS
The Rock Song of our Tomorrow   BILINGUAL EDITION
Translated by David Connolly

Singer-songwriter Dionysis Savvopoulos enjoys an almost mythical status with the Greek public. His language is highly inventive, often zany and surrealistic, and its inherent poetical quality has not been lost on the critics, who classify him among the other leading Greek poets of his generation.

GEORGE SEFERIS   1979 NOBEL PRIZE FOR LITERATURE
Novel and Other Poems   BILINGUAL EDITION
Translated by Roderick Beaton

Often compared during his lifetime to T.S. Eliot, Seferis is noted for his spare, laconic, dense and allusive verse. Seferis better than any other writer expresses the dilemma experienced by his countrymen then and now: how to be at once Greek and modern.

ILIAS VENEZIS
Serenity
Translated by Joshua Barley

The novel follows the journey of a group of Greek refugees from Asia Minor who settle in a village near Athens. It details the hatred of war, the love of nature that surrounds them, the hostility of their new neighbours and eventually their adaptation to a new life.

GEORGIOS VIZYENOS
Thracian Tales
Translated by Peter Mackridge

These short stories bring to life Vizyenos' native Thrace. Through masterful psychological portayals, each story keeps the reader in suspense to the very end: Where did Yorgis' grandfather travel on his only journey? What was Yorgis' mother's sin? Who was responsible for his brother's murder?

GEORGIOS VIZYENOS
Moskov Selim
Translated by Peter Mackridge

A novella by Georgios Vizyenos, one of Greece's best-loved writers, set in Thrace during the time of the Russo-Turkish War, whose outcome would decide the future of southeastern Europe. *Moskov Selim* is a moving tale of kinship, despite the gulf of nationality and religion.

NIKIFOROS VRETTAKOS
Selected Poems
BILINGUAL EDITION
Translated by David Connolly

The poems of Vrettakos are rooted in the Greek landscape and coloured by the Greek light, yet their themes and sentiment are ecumenical. His poetry offers a vision of the paradise that the world could be, but it is also imbued with an awareness of the abyss that the world threatens to become.

AN ANTHOLOGY
Greek Folk Songs
BILINGUAL EDITION
Translated by Joshua Barley

The Greek folk songs were passed down from generation to generation in a centuries-long oral tradition, lasting until the present. Written down at the start of the nineteenth century, they became the first works of modern Greek poetry, playing an important role in forming the country's modern language and literature.

AN ANTHOLOGY
Greek Folk Tales
Translated by Alexander Zaphiriou

Greek folk tales, as recounted throughout Greek-speaking regions, span the centuries from early antiquity up to our times. These are wondrous, whimsical stories about doughty youths and frightful monsters, resourceful maidens and animals gifted with human speech, and they capture the temperament and ethos of the Greek folk psyche.

AN ANTHOLOGY
Rebetika: Songs from the Old Greek Underworld
BILINGUAL EDITION

Translated by Katharine Butterworth & Sara Schneider

The songs in this book are a sampling of the urban folk songs of Greece during the first half of the twentieth century. Often compared to American blues, rebetika songs are the creative expression of people living a marginal and often underworld existence on the fringes of established society.